RIPTIDE

RIPTIDE

•••

Van Hartmann

tP
Texture Press
2016

Published in the United States by
Texture Press
1108 Westbrooke Terrace
Norman, OK 73072

For ordering information,
visit the Texture Press website at
www.texturepress.org

Author photo courtesy of Laurel Peterson
Cover photo: Rebecca Dolber

ISBN-13: 978-0-692-63012-9
ISBN-10: 0-692-63012-0

For Laurel

TABLE OF CONTENTS

ACKNOWLEDGEMENTS

The poems indicated have been published previously in the following locations:

Between What Is and What Is Not (The Last Automat Press, 2010): "Acorns," "Asphalt Roof," "Blood Sport," "Cat's Eyes," "Copperheads," "Drought," "Grand Central Shuttle," "Letting Go," "Mud Season," "On Cow Worship," "On Looking at Nhem En's Photographs," "Planting Hostas," "Safe House," "Sewing a Poem," "Shooting Squirrels," "Smokestack," "Stacking Wood," "Visitation," "Water Dog," "What Is Not," and "Wind"

Confluencia in the Valley: "Mud Season"

Confrontation: "Safe House"

Connotation Press: An Online Artifact: "Copperheads," "Seed Time," "Wind"

The Fourth River: "Cypress Trees," "She Might Have Flown," "Tubers"

Inkwell: "Shooting Squirrels"

Red Wheelbarrow Literary Magazine: "Smokestack"

Slant: "Nevada Test Site"

Verse-Virtual: "Cypress Trees," "Left Behind," "Nevada Test Site," "She Might Have Flown," "Tor House," and "Walking the Lane in Late December"

Winning Writers: "Smokestack"

I

The ocean's lizard tongue has snatched me
whole, gulped me down into its
cold wet belly, then coughed me up,

adrift between the day moon's pale disc
and the hungry floor below, a world away
from where its still loud gullet spews foam,

sucks it back,
spews it out again,
eating at the shore.

When the rip beats back my stroke, I relax,
turn parallel to the coast, seek the calm
outside the channel. When the froth spreads,

I let the current carry me outward,
floating in the midday sun,
lazy as Huck lounging on his raft,

conserving my strength as the ocean
swallows me further into itself,
meandering on my back, watching

contrails thread the sky with silver strands
that blossom into tangled Maenad tresses
tossed by roiling winds fed by thermals

rising off the earth's fat bulge of jungle and
desert spiraling up and round cold slabs of
arctic air that tumble from the north.

A seabird stares down,
black silhouette afloat on the updrafts,
haloed by the sun's bright nimbus,

blankly indifferent, one with the sky,
perched for irony. I laugh, embarrassed,
a man my age diving into gaping surf.

SMOKESTACK

Tapered stile of yellow bricks
embraced by bands of iron
that drip a stain of rust
down fire hardened vertebrae
each four or five feet high,
this spine remains erect
beside a power plant now derelict
with window holes of jagged glass,
collapsing roof, floorboards sinking
beneath a coffin lid of dust.

Try to measure this anomaly:
an aging smokestack against a winter sky
contains an Auschwitz. Even defunct
it spews out ash that will not settle quietly;
the mere looking at it stirs a hundred years
of phantoms: transport trains and ovens,
flames devouring Dresden, gray-white
flakes falling softly over Hiroshima,
napalm and little girls burning,
gulags, death squads, desecrated nuns,
bodies bloating Lake Victoria,
Sarajevo rising through its flue,
skulls like bricks laid neatly by a paddy,
trenches crumbling into graveyards in Verdun,
all we buried in that century
we thought we had escaped.

The smokestack pours out shadows
that don't burden the little girl
I saw wrapped in pink
in a Vermont shoe store
sliding her foot into a metal ruler,

limbs supple, spine erect,
taking her own measure, framing out a self,
announcing through her sunshine smile
at the budding of this new century
that it was good.
She fixed on me, a stranger,
as if searching in a mirror,
demanding confirmation,
demanding irises and daffodils,
demanding soil in which to bloom.

I want to believe in her,
want to know how tall she will grow,
what shape she will take,
how she will measure herself
when she is bent and full of memories,
whether in her time
flaming towers will sear the sky and
human shadows come floating down.

THE CUTTERS

We found the oak at dawn,
catastrophe of limbs
stretched in stony lassitude,
a dying Gaul, eighteen, twenty
bruised segments strewn across the meadow,
unstacked, indecent, like Iraqi dead,
an unfinished chore left
by the cutters until morning.

I remember when the world seemed
crafted of dovetail, tongue, and groove,
part fit snug to part,
segment to segment,
joint to joint,
before that long slow train
began its relentless traverse,
pulling thief after thief after thief,
and piece by piece the morning collapsed,
and something more, something worse.

Now these cutters fly in the night,
armed with wings and weapons,
scanning with unnatural sight.
You'd think that the world would convulse,
that the hapless azaleas
would erupt into anger,
refuse to blossom from grief.
But the world has no memory,
the forsythia, persistent, perennial,
naive, bursts again into springtime,
asks us again to believe.

ON LOOKING AT NHEM EN'S PHOTOGRAPHS
OF KHMER ROUGE PRISONERS

The faces look at me
as they must have looked at him.
Why am I here? Can you help me?

He says, *The duty of the photographer*
was just to take the picture.

I stare into eyes collapsing
into dark ravines
of fear, perplexity, defiance.
If I look too long I lose my balance.
No wonder the photographer
moved them along efficiently,
slipping off their blindfolds,
adjusting the angles of their heads,
snapping his picture,
then processing them on
to beatings, gunshots, slow starvation.

These are simple portraits,
matters of fact. No hooded men
balance on boxes with electrical wires
protruding from limbs. No naked
asses and testicles smeared with feces
mount each other. No damaged corpses
lie wrapped in plastic in a freezer.
Some might even be beautiful.

Number six's silver hair.
hangs flat to bracket a face
of slipped flesh through which
his ancient eyes ask ...what?

What could they ask
of the yet incomprehensible?
His mouth falls in parentheses
around his puckered chin.
His thin grey smock hangs loose
about his sagging shoulders.

Number fifty-five still believes
in youth. He scowls,
adolescent and resentful, hair
tousled with sleep, eyes
fixed and fierce beneath
the bruises on his forehead.

Number two-forty-six
has buttoned her black cotton jacket
to the neck. She squints
as if someone has taken her glasses.
Her infant has been told to behave;
a knitted hat protects it from the cold.

One girl, six or eight years old,
has no number.
The collar of her blouse
spreads wide from her throat
like petals, but one side
is rumpled and askew.
I want to smooth it down,
she is so young and blankly staring,
her head too large, her eyes too wide
for the thin neck and narrow shoulders.
I try to picture her skull
stripped clean of lips, brows, nose, and ears
stacked on stacks of bleached bone.

How will they know who she was
if they don't give her a number?

THANK YOU, MISTER PRESIDENT

for saving us from poetry,
barbaric yawp of needy voices
crowding narrow pens, unruly urges
breaking measured lines,
root that cracks the sidewalk,
frost that heaves the road,
curl and crash of surf,
breach and splash of dolphins,
deep bassoon of whales sounding the abyss,
ice cracking, wind thrashing,
groan of pine bent beneath the snow,
rumble of caribou, gallop of horse,
steady stroke of goose, lazy flap of crow,
arms swinging, hammers pounding,
rip of saw through seasoned wood,
tongues of lovers, legs of runners,
tiny heartbeats in the womb,
schoolrooms full of children laughing,
cacophony of swollen rapids in the spring.

Thank you, Mister President,
for striking up your band,
for giving us a martial meter,
and silencing that mess.
Thanks for beating drums, bugle calls,
smartly snapping flags, tread of tanks,
pulse of rotors, throaty growl of F-16s,
sharp report of rifle shot, machine gun's
tight staccato roll, thud of howitzer
and mortar shell, tympani of bombs
dropped from droning fortresses
invisible at forty thousand feet.

Thank you for the clear decisive crack
of bone and spine,
rhythmic spurt of blood,
shredded arteries,
severed flesh,
convulsive tremor
of someone's brother's dying hand,
and that deeper, slower, silent rhythm
of corpses decomposing in the sand.

ERRATA THIS, BEN FRANKLIN

I see you, Ben, bellied up to your fat stove,
polishing your clever spectacles with
Ma Dame de L'Espoire's silk chemise, taking
the laced arm of *Mon Sieur de la Raison* who,
not yet having met *Citoyen L'Etandard Sanglant*,
observes with giddy pleasure the clean snap
lightening makes against your silver key.

You perched on the narrow pinnacle
of the Enlightenment, all Paris at your feet,
ignoring the dour Reverend Edwards' whisper
from behind the brocaded tapestry that
in time their foot shall slip,
set your sharpened knife to a finely feathered
goose's quill and struck erratum after
erratum from the speckled axe of your life.

It was difficult, I'm sure, with ink
clotting and the hardened protein of the quill
dried and jagged, scratching blemish after
blemish into your rag page, and the *sans culottes*
causing nasty little scuffles in the streets,
the guillotine about to loose its rivers of blood,
the pox still hungry, even after feasting on your son,
that other fever latent in the dark-skinned cargo
those Caribbean ships kept bringing to your harbor.
But you made it look easy, urbane, reasonable,
life's final copy burnished clean.

Two centuries later in this age you helped
unlock, I tap electrons onto glowing screens,
cut and paste errata without crude ink
to blot and blur, access fact and history

in deft strokes, my modern mind enhanced,
all I need now corporate and managed,
that kite and key you flew having soared
beyond your wildest dreams, even to the moon.

But still the manuscript is marred,
still the rabble clamors after bread,
still we hack and claw and write with blood
our blemished biographies, still harbor
poxes large and small, deep burrowed viruses that
leak across the screen to scour and scab the world.
Still the Reverend Edwards whispers in our ear.

TRIANGULATION

A squirrel works the wooded hillside
outside my kitchen window,
shovels full its mouth
with brittle leaves, hauls them
load by load up a dormant oak
to a crotch between two branches
too slender for the nest that, tumor-like,
doubles the circumference of the trunk.

Once, I had a dog, a grateful mongrel
saved from the pound,
that took its place each day on our porch
above a slope of working squirrels.
The dog sat patiently,
doing geometry, inert as fired clay
except for the faintest tremor in its jaw;
a careful eye would see
a trace of drool begin to pool
about its gums and note
its pupils plotting diagrams until
a theorem, fully formed,
sprang from its skull,
and down the hill it shot,
Pythagoras incarnate,
black and white hypotenuse,
some hapless prey scrambling
to complete the line back to the tree
from which it strayed, the meeting
preordained, simple triangulation.

TOR HOUSE
for Robinson Jeffers

Clouds roll off the Pacific,
butt the mountain, break and spill
their dark diagonals
against the western slope.

Had Rembrandt etched this rain
it might have tumbled from the right,
inked striations angled at a village
implied by brief strokes
left of center on the flat horizon;
a squat windmill would spread its arms
against the coming storm,
a boy would lead a cow toward sunlight
that cast its rays from an upper quadrant.

There'd be no flabby face in funny hats,
of course, but some burgher, priest,
or loutish clown suggested by a smudge,
the artist perhaps, slipping into costume.
This would be a civil battle
between water, wind, and fire
waged above a plain of cultivated earth.

But on this shattered coast
where Jeffers built a tower of rock
against the slashing surf,
airborne ocean batters boundaries,
dislodges boulders,
dumps its darkness on the world.

And yet, by some precise economy
the salted valley east of the Sierra

gets no rain. Endless sun bleaches
bones left by rodents and lizards,
preparing them for dust.

Between these two extremes a corridor
pocked with chunks of hardened lava
tells us we are young yet and turbulent.

SEED TIME

A hawk has bothered me all afternoon;
his granite silence lurks on oak limbs

above the feeder. He floats
his heavy bulk from tree to tree,

scanning sparrows, doves, and squirrels
squabbling over seed, brash, brazen devourers,

grabbing their fill, shoving one another
aside, chaos of brown, black and gray,

yet working their way toward some terrible
order: who will eat, who weaken, who will

last the winter, who will linger late
in a patch of sun beneath the hawk?

BLOOD SPORT

We sit afterwards, red clay caking
pebbled soles of boots stomped haphazardly
against the pine planked porch, laces loosened,
wood stove leeching steam from socks, blood
flowing back to toes cramped with frost,
November thawing into bourbon-drenched throats,
brown haze of men's talk, tobacco spit, birdshot,
bragging now on dogs, whose has the surest nose,
holds the tightest point, now comparing
pump guns, side by sides, single shots, automatics.

I want to tell how the first covey
fractured the pewter sky, how I swung,
pulled, pumped, swung and pulled again,
taking two at once, watched their tawny beauty
burst to dust then flutter down the morning mist,
the Remington's mouth and chamber
exhaling hot plumes into gray air,
red casings spent beside my feet,
my dog, black against the autumn rust,
scouring tattered tangles of briar and sticks,
returning twice, mouth wrapped soft
about a parcel of feathers.

I want to tell how by noon
the barrel began to burn, my pouch
distend with quail, some still hot with blood
giving warmth to the small of my back,
how I felt their pulse ebb into mine,
felt autumn dropping into winter,
felt broken brothers falling home.

II

I know this ocean, know
its vectors, winds, and currents,
simple math of energy and mass,

know how to move in concert
with its forces, calmly waiting for the wave
that always comes to take me home.

Untethered, I drift, ebbing outward,
little bubbles of memory breaking the surface,
pleasurable at first, then rolling swells

buffet and disturb, gray currents rising from
gray recesses to crest and glisten, shred and spray
before my grasp, then vanish back to gray.

Thin sheath of self shimmers in the moving sun,
shadow skipping like a flat stone across a pond,
before it settles bright on the water's thin film.

I see my teenaged body tanned and sleek
seeking the perfect point inside the curl,
my laughter bouncing off the foam;

smooth silk of breasts against my naked chest;
thick slush of concrete webbed with bars of steel,
a wall well made, standing sound and sure, like hope.

Then distances grown wide,
silence over years, fissures
I still need to close. Each image

erupts, dissolves, layer after layer
floating off, briefly buoyant,
then sinking into time.

NEVADA TEST SITE

June 24, 1957, 6:02 a.m.
Operation Plumbob: "Priscilla'"
(37 kilotons)

We are headed back to Ohio, black dirt,
green woods, muddy creeks, home once,
now collapsing beneath time and distance,
these trips attempts at excavation,
every year more futile
as the thin thread by which
our parents try to tether us
to uncles, aunts, and cousins,
frays against the massive coastal plate
on which we drift.

Darkness slips off the stern of our fifty-seven Ford
into the western wake where L.A. sank
hours before. The desert leaks its chill
through the window glass. Our sealed pod
slides silent through the Nevada night,
our father's anger subsided,
the family dormant since Barstow.
We stir seed by seed to his crooning
"Tumbling Tumbleweeds," one hand
rhythmically patting our mother's knee, the other
tapping out the tune against the vibrating wheel.

Day is afoot somewhere
down that long tube our headlights cut
out of the gray slate of the eastern sky,
day aborning, laying down a rail-straight highway
of shimmering concrete and gun barrel heat,
Vegas by breakfast, Great Salt Lake by nightfall.

You choose this moment to burst into being
above the yuccas, the sagebrush, the flat subservient
sand, slip your little apocalypse into the narrow
space between the last remnant of night
and the thickening dawn, steal a shard
from the sun to crack apart the horizon,
a flash that spreads a white stain
then contracts to a chrysanthemum
of a hole that hangs just long and low enough
against the northern sky
to sear your image onto my retina.

Late in life our father will protest,
he never hit our mother.
We will somewhat agree,
recalling whirlwinds of words
from across the seat of a car,
a kitchen table, spilling through a bedroom door,
that swept the sound from her mouth,
reduced her, having found some mantra
that worked a salve around her hurt,
to a flat and wordless humming,
a stubble of herself.

I am twelve, have just begun to sprout
a map of sinews, muscles, veins,
have not yet found a voice
within my strange unstable throat,
too young to know the cause
of that howling wind that can erupt
from a man who can coax a bluebird
to take a peanut from his open palm.

But I wake on the cusp
of this June morning
to your dawning,
scramble for the radio

where a rush of desert static
confirms your birth.
When day comes,
it rises on the other side
of your white flame.
The thread has snapped,
the journey twisted back
onto itself, the road
a fist that grasps the universe
in tight concentric circles.

TUBERS

Snot and dirt, I recall, crusted
in the ruins of his blue jeans, dried
flowerets of mucous against a purple sky,

maybe some blood, and black loam
sweet with earth stink carried from a farm
far away where beans or corn or apples,

pears or acres of alfalfa,
waited for their harvest while he lay curled
at our feet taunting through his sobs: *Hit me.*

So we planted knotted fists like tubers
in the furrows of his flesh. I was nine.
It was late September. School had begun.

He had come among us, sullen, defiant,
fated by his dirt-streaked face, shattered clothes,
to linger like a stray outside our camp.

Vagabond, itinerant, words
some smart classmate brought from home,
hung on him like a battered shield.

It wasn't his unwashed neck, frayed T-shirt
gray with wear, or even the way his eyes
searched the ground for a pathway out.

It was the smell, a faint scent
of family, of tribe, of otherness,
acrid and sweet, that excited and repelled

our young limbs tanned by summer,
newly elongated, pent with power,
wanting to be tested and heroic.

He said, *You can hit me*, dared my friend and me,
standing in the field I had helped my parents plant.
You can hit me, he said. *My daddy does. You can too.*

My friend went first. I followed, cursed the kid
when he smirked, cursed when he asked for more,
his eyes rimmed with red desire, thick sob-laughs

mocking from his mouth, we striking haphazardly,
bewildered by his ache, bewildered by
his low flat moans, planting blows that would grow

large and deep through the years, sowing this
harvest of tubers until the sun dropped and
evening came with a chill strange and new.

When we finished, I scanned the hill to my house
for fear my mother had seen, for fear
she would tell my father I'd run off like the calf

that had bolted in a storm whom we found
wild-eyed and wasted a world away.

BLIGHT

Here comes that woman,
gray hair shooting tendrils and sparks,
who followed me up Bird Road,
stood at the foot of the front field
spewing locusts and crows across the golden rod,
screaming shrill caws that I stole her dog.
No use my protesting it followed me
skipping, scampering between my wheels,
no use explaining I tried to shoo it home,
had a dog already, didn't need hers.

Strange how she still follows me,
culling the guilt she planted
when I was nine years old
pedaling greeting cards door to door.
She seemed even then to know
I longed to split apart the ripened melons
just to see their sweet juice flow,
lap it like a wolf after a long hunt,
seemed to know I dreamed
of climbing down the cherry tree that
rubbed against my bedroom window
to prowl the countryside at night,
and that the following winter
I would take my young cousin
to tiptoe gingerly across the barely
hardened ice on a neighbor's pond.

At least she's not the one who
placed order after order to keep me
returning to her darkly shuttered parlor,
thinking I was her dead son
come home at last from the war,

grabbing at my wrist, pulling me
to photos on the mantle of my shadow self
in uniform, filling my little bank with debt
absolute and nonnegotiable.

That's the one who raised
the red-winged blackbirds
from their new nests in the tall grass
to dive like furies at my wide-eyed head,
leaving scars that stick like aphids.

FAMILY PORTRAIT

They stand in dark suits,
sentinels confronting the camera,
except my father, shortest,
second from the right, head dropped,
shoulders hunched, scowling from
beneath his brow. Four brothers
home in Ohio for their mother's funeral,
their father pasted blank and flat
into the center, bewildered
by that new thing he's become,
a widower.

I try to read my father's posture.
Was there an argument?
Was he angry at the artifice
of this posed portrait?
Or, was this the family role
we didn't see in the world
he built with us? Was he
the runt, the butt, the outsider?
Is that wary youth the cocoon
in which was stirring the man we knew?

Questions a son can't ask a father,
nor why, when I find a faded photo
of my older brother and me, six years old,
padded down in winter wool, clutching
freshly packaged pencils, papers, crayons,
waiting for the school bus on a cold Ohio morning,
I see the same scowl beneath the same
lowered brow cradling the man in me.

SHOOTING SQUIRRELS

Shoot a rabbit, it expires
of shock, quick hop, puff of fur,
gone before it lands,
eyes fixed and brown, sometimes
not even a spot of blood
against the glove-like pelt.

Squirrels die hard,
full of rodent teeth and claws
clinging to bark, breaking branches
as they fall, scrambling
even when they hit the ground
from thirty-five or forty feet.

That takes the beauty out of killing,
having to track them down,
shoot them once, twice again,
staring deep inside their
desperate pissed off eyes.

COPPERHEADS

Summer came late,
spring spilling down
the length of June,
little waves of green run wild,
pooling drunk
and leaving me
marooned and mute,
almost like sleep.

That was the summer
we didn't argue
about the chores.
It was the summer
of silence
packed inside a rising weight
of northbound boxes
with promises
we feared we wouldn't keep.

You went about your work
as if across a floor
too thin to bear the tremor
in your voice
when I explained
again
the logic of our choice.

When at last
the sun struck,
pounding steam
from besotted growth,
distilling stalks and tendrils
tipped to probe
the freshly opened air,

July uncoiled in swirls
that broke like fists
against the house.

I stared
on toward August,
half already boxed
and sealed,
unable to return
or yet to go,
knowing
you did nothing wrong
except not be
who I kept wanting
you to be.

At length
a need for ballast
sent me out
to try to put
our long delinquent yard,
its freight of endless rain
and mounds of heat,
in order.

A tarp lay bent
beneath a crust
of last year's autumn,
black brown leaves
fermenting back to humus
wedged between
the porch and mower.

When I pulled it back
I saw them
twisting in the sudden light
as if the fifth day
had dawned

with warmth
and wariness
into this breaking world.

Slick and silken things,
they stirred newborn in coiled
bands of oiled rust and taupe,
some dozen lemon-yellow tails,
mud-flat heads,
each body finger-thick,
half a forearm long,
writhing and unwrapping,
glistening blank malevolence
awake to meet the sun.

So this was life,
a kind of hope
that rose
as if from earth itself,
inherited with poisons
from past lives
bitten with desire.

It was late August when I killed them,
packed their venom into boxes
headed north.

WIND

Wind spills off the plains
like the soft lap of lake surf
on summer nights,
silent except for a low hum
that delivers a persistent pressure
to eardrums and organs,
causing folk to bend ever so slightly
to the tilt of the day.

Further south it has curled about itself,
tight muscles, lifting, clawing, dropping
objects and living things.

We have a smallness within us,
you and I, that puffs and thrashes
against the cage we've built around it.
Mine prowls the house,
kicks at papers,
punches holes in the Vivaldi,
sends little devils spinning
across the polished pine,
causing the dog to twitch in her sleep.

On those days I tighten the screws
around the storm doors,
double caulk the windows,
and crank up the music
for fear of letting mine loose
on the world
at the same time as yours.

III

I feel my warmth steal out into the vast
sump of sea, that slow relentless siphon;
a lulling lethargy quiets my legs and arms.

I hear some land bird sing to me with
full-throated ease from the deep woods
of some distant continent,

dividing its ancient scale into
peaks and valleys, dales and hills,
trilling its ti so la, *and* do mi re,

again and again, chanting perhaps Chinese,
ni hao ma, ni hao ma, *beckoning,*
then demanding that I obey the god

who spreads through this salt blood
rising and falling about me, unyielding mass
in which I float with lips and faith now parching.

Then a snap of anger, not at this,
this can still be managed, but at
the other bird that hangs against the dull blue sky,

sliding its scar back and forth across the sun,
observing, its silence loud with mockery.
I sense some wrongness in its lingering,

wonder if its flat black eye can pierce
the swirls of opaque fluid to conjure
nameless things alive beneath my dangling limbs,

creatures cold and coiling, summoning
childhood fears of letting hands and feet
hang exposed outside the covers.

I shake off those thoughts,
take control, as I always have,
determined I will not die.

VISITATION

Your laughter comes and goes
like the moon
that awakened me at four a.m.
staring wide-eyed through my
open window,
a light beyond the screen
that contracted and grew,
a pulsing wave as thick as matter,
like gravity, that pulled my sight
into its spreading form,
until I gasped and ruptured it.

Up rose a tawny head,
a deer whose coat had caught
the moon's full face
and fed it to my soul.
Its startled gaze fixed on mine,
brown depths immeasurable,
then off it shot, a particle of light
shrinking into the night,
sharp hooves striking a fading echo,
the memory of your laugh,
against the summer ground.

LETTING GO

You stapled eyes
to things
I couldn't see.
Hard task,
to pry those rivets loose,
not knowing if what
they stabbed stayed stuck
or fell away with you.

So tell me,
do the dying make apologies,
seek confirmation?
Do they ask forgiveness
or merely to be left alone?

Was it a mirror you watched
as you undressed for death?
Did you ask God
to set your hair,
compose your mind,
shut down your eyes,
prepare your soul
for letting go?

That blank
bewildered
distant look,
was that yours
or mine?

SYMPATHY CARD

There are no comparisons
for grief. Each well closes

round its corpse, plumbed by its
own line from living to dead.

Into each a survivor falls
out of time into the mute

absolute of loss. Each must
find the footholds back,

grasp at fistfuls of light,
listen for the world's music,

climb up into the daily
rotation of the earth,

rebirth arriving for each
with its own impossible dawn.

SANDING IT SMOOTH

This red oak, its rivulets of grain
sanded, stained, and sealed,
would finish off the cabinet
I've been at for years.
I hold the board to the light,
discover a slight blemish,
and run my fingers down its surface.
They trip over something coiled and knotted,
a defect I could fix with a sheet of sandpaper
wrapped tight about a block of wood.
I let my fingers linger over its hint
of something living once inside,
a tendril or a root, perhaps a serpent
petrified, or some nymph out of Ovid,
some slender lover fleeing forever
fixed beneath the bark that sheathed
the wood from which this plank was milled.

I stroke it gently as I did your smooth
belly when the doctor grabbed my hand,
pressed it hard against your flesh,
matter-of-fact bastard that he was, and said,
Feel that? Again, I run my fingers
across the lumpy ridge and trace
the knotted cord coiled beneath.
That's the cancer. It's come back,

I toss the board and once again
fail to finish the cabinet.

That was the closest I ever felt to you,
touching that thing growing
wild inside, some excess of your

own self rebelling to coil about
and devour the rest, I yearning to
sand it smooth but knowing my tools
were inadequate, so taking you instead
into my arms to let your belly merge
with mine as that rogue root shot out
a shoot to enter me and join us
into one doomed vine wrapped tree.

STROKE SPEECH

Stroke-wrecked, he stumbles
back toward language,
simple sounds tumbling
sideways, slipping inside out.
He falls mute, sets out again,
voice teetering like a toddler's
first steps. A sentence sags
like an ancient bridge
hollowed by rust and rot;
girders convulse and collapse,
no longer able to bear
the weight of thought.

She feeds him consonants
and vowels at the kitchen table,
baby spoons of labials,
fricatives, glottal stops;
all dribble out a drool of mutterings
until she pounds her open palm
against the wood, a primal beat
born of weariness, frustration,
and stumbles into rhythm.

I want pancakes for breakfast.

A phrase forms coherent and whole,
little miracle of speech,
deep music beneath the shell of words.

LARES

My father lifts a pewter ashtray
cast in high school metal shop,
gray cat's face, flat articulated whiskers,
pointed ears, recessed feline eyes, little tongue
pushing through lips, sets it down,
picks up a palm-sized silver crescent wrench
his father bought at the age my son might be,
then a pocket knife my mother's father
gave him when they finally made their peace,
its walnut handle blackened with the years.

These and other amulets and fetishes
crowd the table, line the walls, fill the floor,
house the *lares* of our tribe: Grandfather's tongs
used to carry ice; two straight-edged razors
mounted in a shadow box, bright steel
against a field of felt; draftsman's penciled drawing
of piston, rod, and gears for a transport ship
that got my father his deferment from the War;
handmade cedar chest; reconditioned desk;
photograph of him smiling sheepish proud
beside a dented thirty-seven Packard
spun across a sheet of ice.

In the garage: the band saw and lathe
his doctor no longer lets him use;
shortwave radio kept alive since the fifties;
upright freezer hauled from Ohio,
now filled with frozen lemon cubes
for *margaritas* he no longer drinks.

He worries over what will happen to these
gods he's guarded all these years,

waves his hand across the room, blind priest
blessing a fleet about to embark for distant lands,
and asks me what I want.

I want for him to see my face,
hear my voice, follow our conversation;
want to see him sitting at his workbench
carving blocks of wood, fixing ancient radios,
not knowing how to say he loves us
except through what he makes.

I take the pewter cat and penciled piston,
lares good enough, I guess, for now.

SHE MIGHT HAVE FLOWN

Through the frosted window I watched
a little girl step out from beneath
my mother's years, hooded in a parka
and grinning, her unsteady foot
probing the black tire that hung
on a brittle rope from a white birch
in the middle of the meadow
coated with an early snow.
Why I watched instead of calling out
a warning, I don't know.
I think I hoped that makeshift swing
might lift her to whatever she had seen
that made her eyes go wide with wonder.

Perhaps it was some childhood memory
hung from an aged oak rising from Montana
wheat where all the sisters she has lost
pushed one another to the sky.

Perhaps it was my father,
whom she couldn't lift
from the earth to which he fell,
for which she blamed herself,
as those left behind will do,
and thought, *if only I'd had this,*
or *maybe if I can master it*
I'll lift him now.

Perhaps I read it wrong,
looking from my window
on that cold Vermont afternoon,
my elderly widowed mother
wanting *to go for a walk by myself,*

to probe the snow-wrapped meadow
and its secrets unencumbered.

Perhaps, as she slipped her foot
into the ring of that old black tire
suspended on a dubious tether of
frayed hemp she whispered
to her long-dead daddy,
to my new-dead father,
to me and all the men whose
angry logic had kept her grounded,
Watch me fly now
on my own wings
beyond the grip of gravity,
beyond the rule of logic,
beyond those laws that I at eighty-six
have every right to break.

When she fell I felt a grief so full
it made me furious at the world
of fact and at myself for not
attending better to things like
ropes and time and memories.

CYPRESS TREES

That's the way it happens.
You're sitting in a wheelchair
and your head isn't right,
and the cypress trees outside the window,
whipped by a hot desert wind,
are doing their savage dance
looking every bit like sex,
and the nurse doesn't answer the call button
and has a Spanish name you can't remember,
and he's a handsome young man
who tried to climb into your bed
last night, and you know he wants to
do things that are wrong, although
your daughter says he wouldn't really want
you with legs that don't work and a head
that's not right, but you correct her
because you know how pretty you were
once and how you once were wanted,
so you call out, *Help me! Please,*
someone help me, because your eyes
have stopped working and your
head isn't right and your shoulders
are cold and your legs won't move
and the nurse with the Spanish name
hasn't come and the cypress trees
are dancing like you did when you
were young, and you hear an old woman
cry out, *No, no. Wait, Mama, please wait,*
but you're not sure if it was her or was
your head that isn't right, and the cypress
trees are thrashing and struggling to rise
into the blue cathedral of the sky
but they are tangled in their roots,

and you feel their frenzy because
your legs won't work and they've
asked you to dance like you did as a girl
with hair that flew like starlings and
hands that moved like the breeze
and hips that rose like the ocean
in the hot thirsty wind of your youth.

LAZARUS RISING

Miracle! Dappled coat that flutters
in the breeze, flood of light that strikes
knives into my newly sighted eyes.

Dogwood blossoms, bleeding white
across the thick green greed of resurrected
grass, drift and melt toward summer.

My skin has split its winter's shell,
soaks up the cruelty of this season.
Veins convulse to the surge of blood,

sweet sleep cracked open,
naked life tumbling out,
red and raw and bruising.

Desire barely put to rest
awakens, grows ripe like swollen
peaches, aching taste of lust –

for that lovely lace of newly opened
leaf that filters the spring's warm sun,
for that purple burst of rhododendron,

for the stroke of the wind against my face,
for the sudden shock of scent, those lilacs,
someone somewhere baking bread –

spins my head like wasps abuzz with
venom. Dark thoughts at last subdued
break out like running sores, scabs

torn off with the unwrapping of the shroud.
And that unwrapping. My wife stared,
wide-eyed with fear, for me, perhaps

of me howling like a kid whose dam
had dropped him out into this thorn
pocked bramble blasted world of woe.

My children's faces, once white petals
free of grief, now agape like fresh dug graves,
I see them mirroring me and want to weep.

Now I'll have to watch them stoop,
grow brittle, brown with rust, see
even my youngest mix with earth.

I didn't ask for this, again to stumble
through the blank closing down of sight,
ears ringing into silence, terror of delusions,

mean spite of an old man's fears,
all this decay and death to do again
for that young trickster selling his
dope, his irresistible poison, hope.

ON/OFF

Maybe a simple switch
like the one by my bed I reach for
when I've finished reading or
a toggle like the one beneath
the frame of my table saw.

Definitely not a dimmer, where
light fades slowly, leaving me
to trip about in the twilight
as my father did, chanting
memories in the half-light
that refused to let him go, as he did
when he complained about the Filipinos
at the dialysis center who talked
around him in Spanish, as he did
when he pounded his cane angrily
into the pine planks of the dining room
floor, calling out my mother's name
again and again and again when she
was slow to bring his coffee.

And not that slow stumbling descent
through which she now stares,
her husband gone, convinced some
dark-haired man has been entering
her room at night to touch her,
and not that fumbled clutching
at the wrong end of her spoon,
to scoop at the air beside her pureed
potatoes and stab the silver handle
backwards into her cheek, and not
that slipping coyly from her wheelchair,
parked by the nursing home staff
in the hallway with a dozen others,

only to land against its sharp frame,
then with a confused grin to scan
the red fluid that spreads across her arm,
calling out to the nurse that doesn't come,
calling out to the daughter and sons
who can't hold her safe from every
shadow of the spreading darkness,
calling out for someone please just to shut it off.

No, not a dimmer, and probably not
a toggle switch I might accidently
flip in my sleep, but a button labeled
Escape or Delete installed between
my second and third ribs, hidden
beneath my bicep and recessed
so as not to interfere with exercise,
but within easy reach by one good hand,
skin colored and nearly invisible
so as not to frighten my wife.

IV

Something in me dissolving,
I float round to face the endless swells
the ghost moon has summoned,

Face and scalp sere and swollen,
stump of stubble on a blighted field.
Beneath, I hang in liquid space,

lifted and dropped, toes seeking
purchase against the deep until
numbness consumes my calves and thighs.

Again, I try to focus, fighting sleep,
try to count the undulation of the hours,
stuck on those already lost as I drift out,

a speck slipping on this current,
time congealed into a single viscous present,
trapped in mad exchange with that infernal bird

now screaming, rocking
in the center of the sun.
I hear it laugh

as my fist breaks
the surface of a swell

to strike it from the sky.

I subside. Foolish, wasting heat.
Let it leer and babble,
stupid beast.

WHAT IS NOT

Birds flying into glass
drop
beneath the windowed bridge
that arcs the path I walk each day,
absorbed in what I have
or have not done amiss,
causing me to trip
upon the latest littering
of tufted carcasses,
yellow, green, mottled charcoal,
tawny brown,
lying like a pestilence
shaken loose from trees.

I tiptoe past a pair
of tar-deep eyes
that stare into the seeds of things
as mirrors might do
and wonder
what completes that space
between what is and what is not,
the gap that absence opens,
filled by yearning,
perhaps my poem's voice
mouthed like breath
against a skein of dust.

LOOKING FOR DAISY

Lost in Louisville, looking for Daisy's
bourbon lips and golden voice, stalking
the Seelbach, hoping to eavesdrop on Scott

and Zelda before the catastrophe,
I spy a man more like Tom in a mirror
sipping a martini with Myrtle, her

laugh a clatter of quarters tumbling down
the big oak bar. I'm tempted to gather
them up, but it's Daisy I want,

her voice, her touch, perhaps one long
strand of golden hair left behind
to drape across my naked skin.

I walk to the river, watch coal barges
labor the Ohio, scow after scow
piled black with impending fire, the innards

of mountains further east strung like onyx,
cutting currents into currents, trailing
mud brown eddies layered with swirling silt.

I skip a quarter across the river's surface
then ask where it began, the coal, the thick
dark water, the soil it carries, the memory torn
from Eden that weighs on my heart like gold.

LEFT BEHIND

The sermon was about hens folding chicks
beneath their wings, protecting their brood from

a cloven-hooved fox who prowled craftily
within the smiles of richly robed Pharisees.

The censer flooded the nave with smoke that
climbed the shafts of light in spreading feathers

of red and blue and gold. The priest
opened his arms to form a cross,

let fall a downy white surplice, linen
and silk, and beckoned, while grim-faced deacons

beat the pews for timid parishioners,
my wife among them, who fled to the altar,

took bread and wine where the thick stone wings
of the transept embraced the huddled flock.

I hung back, left behind,
scanning the nave for the fox.

DROUGHT

Thirty years of distance packed into this visit,
each outing blossoms like a dormant
pod evolved to weather drought.

This one takes us to the sheep
that in this sere time can only eat or drink
what men haul in by flatbed four by four.

We navigate a stark terrain of jolts and slippages,
jostling sacks of oats and tanks of sloshing
water destined for earth encrusted troughs.

The moment is thick with all
we haven't said in over thirty years.
It takes an hour to find the sheep

huddled beneath the scattered shade
of eucalyptus not yet stolen
by kangaroos and midday sun.

Caked with dust, they seem mere
mounds of fired mud pressed hard
against the red brown dirt,

until they see or hear the truck. Then
they stir, lean, cascade down the rock
pocked slope, gathering mass and speed,

as if we ourselves were gravity
pulling this avalanche of muscle,
bone and wool upon ourselves.

I steer and shift, fumble at foreign knobs,
try to avoid catastrophe, as sacks knifed open
spill a golden stream of oats across the hillside.

We escape the onslaught,
but not perhaps that other urgency
that drought can yield,

a parched and hollow hunger
that tumbles down our lives
to bury those who feed us.

WALKING THE LANE IN LATE DECEMBER

The stream complains from the ravine's
deep hollow, swollen eddies and whorls,
Stravinsky score of quavers and clefs,
at its heavy freight of frost compressed,
convulsed, breaking free to tumble toward the sea.

Houseguests saunter up ahead, arms loose
as summer, swinging to some sweet melody,
Mozart or Joplin, eyes adrift on the cloudless sky,
dazzled out of time by the bright white
magic of the day swirling into improvisation.

I linger behind, plant each boot into winter,
head bent, finding familiar frets in the path,
holding my arms close, seeking my center,
lower my body's weight onto the full of my feet,
careful not to skid, not to rush the tempo,
not to land off balance onto the thick slick
ice beneath the freshly fallen snow.

Above, a gray brown thatch of maple and beech
stripped clean of green inscribes a tangled staff
against the sun. A hawk floats on the breeze,
in tune with the season and hungry.

A muffled crack sings across the snow,
distant branch, hunter's rifle, a bone, or
the conductor's baton impatient
at our failure to read his score.

One of my friends has gone down.
Nothing broken except
the illusion of the snow's soft fluff.

Where his fall has swept the ice clean,
an opaque mirror stares up like zinc
or tarnished silver or the flat gray
eye of the hawk, his hood removed,
somber as Brahms, dark as eternity.

SNOW DAY

Found time is found money,
magical as the snow that has
blotted out the day.

Bright white coins
amass in Midas heaps
making roads impassible,

canceling business,
encasing the house
in drifts of sunlit wealth.

How to spend this windfall?
Pay off old debts
or buy new fun?

Paint the bathroom,
fix the drip beneath the sink,
grade a stack of papers,

finally organize my taxes?
I lace up my boots,
take the dog into the deep woods,

grow a snout like his,
burrow into soft mounds
of winter's frozen scent,

made mad by remnants
of pine and deer and squirrel,
together dancing wild and snapping

at the swirling flakes, squandering
all my treasure tumbling down
this hole the day has opened up in time.

MUD SEASON

This month-long regurgitation of the earth
has felled a birch bowed low by winter's
weight. It's shed its coat of snow and settled
softly to catch a backward glimpse of roots
spoking skyward from the clotted soil
spread wide to drink the warm spring rain.

Rocks are moving on the mountain,
rising like the dead at Judgment Day,
some, like loaves rolled smooth and baked
by glacial tides ten thousand winters past,
now cast upon the flooded April; others,
jagged teeth broke loose from the earth's
deep jaw, push through thaw, cut the mud's
soft gum, breach the new green ground,
hungry for the sky, forgetting
they aren't fire, air, or water, but rock.

Mud will do that, push up things long buried,
roots and rock and banished thoughts,
turn the world upside down for a time
until it settles back into place.

Later, I'll take the chain saw and slice
the birch into segments. I'll dig out
some rocks with a shovel, lay them flat
for the back steps I'll build this summer.
Most I'll leave in place as evidence of
the capriciousness of gravity,
the trickery of the spring.

MELVILLE'S CHOLA WIDOW
JUMPSTARTS TIME

Cast upon enchanted islands,
wrapped in paralytic grief,
Hunilla lifts a stick against
the breakers that fling their crystal
gloss across the flattened sand
that takes it in, darkens, leaks it
back into the mouth that curls
again to spew new gloss
across the sand that once again
will leak it back into that mouth
that swallowed husband, brother, time,
this being perhaps hell's eternity,
sobbing flux of particle and wave
bent and pushed and pulled
by unseen moons,
always different, still the same.

Hunilla lifts her wand,
cuts a notch,
calls it *Now*,
finds a place to stand
in time.

READING DON QUIXOTE

Old man, I summon you,
tilting at specters spun from your
word-wracked brain, Sancho's bulk
abandoned chapters back to sleep off
mutton and sangria, Dulcinea's hips
shimmering somewhere past the curved page
I now crest, you spurring Rosinante
over ink-spattered pulp as I charge
down toward the shadow of a dark
spine congealed of thread and glue.

The white page shines beneath
an avalanche of particles,
smaller than atoms, that pierce
the hand that holds this book,
photons, neutrinos, chaos of collisions
hurled by Mother Sun
to lighten her mass, cascading
through and corrupting ours,
delicately balanced in the battle
between energy and matter.

Old man, I summon you
from fields of flattened pulp
that curve like space and time
flowing into each other, light
warping as it passes the stars,
call you forth from particles
of ink and thought to tilt
at the darkness, armed
with the glitter of words
flung from dead trees spewing sparks
to ignite brains like ours,
flammable tinder, brittle brush.

V

Porous sheath of skin now giving way
to ocean seeping in, mingling
with my blood and blood of unseen creatures

deconstructing me, I must draw boundaries,
establish definitions, push the impertinent world
back into its proper spheres.

I start mouthing syllables through cracked
and salted lips, name names as Adam did
until they coalesce into prayer.

But a weariness I've never known
imposes silence. How many hours
have gone? What heat is left?

The sun has slipped,
sits bloated and bloodied
as if some savage feast

has left it sated and yawning
above the ocean's golden lap,
inviting me to sleep.

I look for the bird —
a point, at least,
by which to measure

where and who I am,
surprised to find
a need for it, like thirst.

It has gone, its flat black eye
attracted to some other speck
floating in the sea.

PLANTING HOSTAS

I think about the deer,
as I watch my aged neighbors
set out half a dozen plants.
Across the road, a wooded enclave
teems with hungry Bambis.
Those hostas won't survive the spring.

He proceeds with pecking strokes,
boney arms barely raising
the narrow beak of a shovel
to chip brown earth into perfect holes;
she, stronger in the legs, but
now weak of mind, bends,
lifts the knotted roots,
then kneeling, lowers them
with a crooning sound,
as one might lay the past to rest
or plant a promise for the future.

She scoops in dirt in even measures.
He drags a hose from behind the house,
transformed into a laden dray
leaning at his husbandry,
lets water spill into the dented ground
that rings each shock of newborn green.
She pats fresh soil atop the wet,
then grips the spade he steadies as a staff
to lift her body back to air.

Joining hands, they set their feet
against the earth and dance
slow steps around each plant.
I say nothing that might jinx whatever
incantation they chant against the deer.

KEY WEST

It's springtime,
an hour before dawn. Roosters strut like
puffed up bags of autumn; swollen throats of red,
brown, yellow, blue, and rust stretch for the sky.
Orphans of history, they scream out the morning,
fish bones of fractured light caught in their gullets,
coughed into day.

Their clogged alarum
summons a jumbled past of pirates, conquistadors,
green black mangrove forests spotted white by egrets,
pink queen conch, koi ponds, six-toed cats, coral fans
dancing in the tide. Submerged remnants of a half-
remembered isle coalesce, break apart, fill the alleys
with visions.

Refugees from
a cold wet north, we've come, orphans of our
past, to ask this land to rock us back to wholeness.
Neglectful, indifferent, we've allowed our selves
to crumble and fall away like fragments
scattered across the ocean floor where living reefs
once grew.

Last night
we lay in the aftermath of our pleasure,
cast upon a shore of dreams, our past opaque
like silver tarpon suspended in the swells,
magnified by some trick of sunlight and water,
almost within reach, then with a shiver of fins,
vanished.

Cayo Hueso
the Spanish called this island of bones
strewn across rock and sand and coral.
What those bones dreamed before they broke
and bleached to white is lost, unless the roosters,
puffed up clarions of the dawn,
summon it from their gullets.

GRAND CENTRAL SHUTTLE

No one meets your smile.
Disgorged from subway cars,
they slither sideways, thin eyes
grasping at the ground, scatter, recombine,
tumble down the concrete sluice
of shadows, seepage, urine,
backpacks bobbing, clipping shoulders,
Sorry, Fuck you, caught in throats.
At intervals, rumbling shrieks of steel,
bursts of air compressed from moving trains,
convulse the tunnel, push the tide along.

Around a bend,
Pip pop pippity pop.

A young man rides an upturned crate,
skitters across the grime;
beneath a hoodie, limbs
protrude, fists flail, sticks
beat on buckets, pots, and pans,
roasting rack, brake drum, twenty gallon tubs
retrieved from alleys, dumpsters, curbs,
the world of light above.

*Ba dop ba dop ka ching ching
ka rack ka rack ka pang.*

Gloved claws pound at rubber,
steel, and rusted iron; bits of hardware
bounce and skip into the air;
The little god bounces after them,
with spindly legs and arms;
decaying metal, fraying plastic,

alloys decomposing into ore,
beaten back to life, now float
with him an inch above the ground.

A crowd has pooled around this man
whose face emits a joyous rage,
dreadlocks flaring, brows contracted,
eyes half shuttered, fool's smile,
flopping hood, coil of blue around his
pulsing neck, arms a blur of flaming
spirals dancing into space.

*Ka chink ka chunk ka chinkity chank
ta ting ta ting ta tang.*

The drummer hammers at my bones,
sternum, rib cage, skull.
The man beside me taps his foot;
a woman sways her hips.
I smile across the floating world,
see Shiva smiling back.

WATER DOG

My dog stands joint deep
in a shallow stream;
her greedy engine tongue
dips, curls, flips, and laps
an ocean down her gullet.
Beneath her dripping chest
more water rambles by
in search of dragonflies or deer,
chortling toward ponds and rivers,
and on, assured the sun
will lift it from the Atlantic,
drop it back on Bromley Mountain
to tumble down that ravaged face
of rivulets and gullies
to where my dog will stand
still gulping,
if not this season then the next.

ASPHALT ROOF

The neighbor's new metal roof
announces itself beyond the pines.
Joyful, clean and red through
frequent storms, it gives the snow
no purchase, uses simple laws of physics,
mass and weight and pitch,
to shuck each burden as it comes.

My roof stays white all winter;
its shingles, little asphalt fingers,
clutch the snow like anxious lovers.
Ice dams the gutters, behind it
a glacier forms; beneath its cap,
detritus lingers: pine needles, seed pods,
acorns, leaves, and bark, shells of crickets,
locusts, wasps, bits of nest and feather,
crumbling flakes of plaster
from the chimney that needs repair.
This baggage works its way between the flaps,
gives access to decay encased by piling snow
that blankets deeper damage still
to plywood, beams, and joists.

Sometimes I ask the man who plows my drive
to rake the roof: two hundred bucks a shot;
the price of therapy; similar results.
I stand back and watch the avalanche,
startled by the crash, half expect to see
a prehistoric hunter tumble all intact,
or fragments of parchment sealed in urns,
pieces of my past. When he's done,
I check the clean gray slope,
poke about the weight it's shed,
feel briefly whole.

FIDDLEHEADS

The dog, wild with scent,
bounds ahead, leaving me
to feel my way through thick
kaleidoscopes of needle, leaf, and bark,
struck as much by sudden shafts of early light
as by any plant or animal I could name.
Careening from smell to smell,
she keeps me tethered to the path
which she traverses and expands,
disappearing through culverts and lesions
in the wall of fir that all but swallows her,
the forest floor resounding from her paws,
earth a skin stretched tight
across a frame of rock and fallen log,
until she emerges, panting, watching,
waiting for me to come.

You lie curled in bed with the cat,
working on our relationship.
Already we vie for ownership of
pockets of domestic space;
debate definitions of things
like *kindling*, you arguing for
those spindly shoots I called *twigs*
you glean from the plot where
you prepare your garden, I
demanding narrow shanks of timber
split with an axe; ownership of doorways
where I mount my chin-up bar,
turn your *home* into a *gym*;
ownership of the morning,
my *music* cluttering your silence with *noise*;

ownership even of the dog, who sits for hours
balanced and watchful between us.

But at this early hour the dog is mine.
I follow her down this trail
that cuts a tangent against the meadow
behind the house, then caroms north,
sinking into hemlock, maple, beech, and birch,
climbing shale, slate, and wavy sheets of schist,
rippling its rugged spine clear up to Canada,
my gaze fixed on vertebrae of root and stone,
slippery ribs of fallen trees, wondering
if Emerson had this in mind, egoism
stripped by fear of slipping in the muck,
anxious that an ankle bone could crack,
with only the dog to run for help.

I wish I knew these woods
as the dog knows them,
without this satchel of words
I tote like a tourist, fumbling
to match the pictures in my *Audubon*
with tufts of green erupting from the forest floor,
stuck to my book like a schoolboy
struggling with declensions,
yet enchanted by the names men have given:
Staghorn, Horsetail, Goldilocks,
comely two-toned moss that traipses
curly-haired and carefree across the shaded ground;
Dame's Rocket, womanly, elegant,
purple with desire; monkish hooded
Jack-in-the-Pulpit, preaching futilely
to *Skunk Cabbage, Buckthorn, Witch Hazel*,
and all the swaying ferns.

Ahead a clearing tries to open,
dank brown earth punctured with new born

fiddleheads, pale green spirals tightly curled
inside cocoons of gray muslin, each
a chambered nautilus in reverse, lush and leafy
futures pending, pushing, soon to bob on the breeze
like the hair that will fall about your neck
when you unwrap yourself from sleep.
Along the clearing's edge a wall runs low,
slate and granite slabs laid onto each other
by some farmer two centuries gone
marking off his property, trying to tame this
rock-strewn earth into furrows lined and tilled
in even sunlit rows, producing golden corn or oats,
grazing Scottish sheep or English heifers,
now cracked apart by slender maple saplings,
the field long-since repossessed by seedlings,
the ferns connected underground by rope-like
tendrils, slippery brown clotted web of life.

It's late spring and the woods exude
pine and humus born of snow melt and mud,
the scent bewitching me and the dog,
enticing us to press on past the rising heat
into recesses dark and cool as night.
I stop to sink my fingers beneath the skin,
clutch that web of pulsing veins
on which I walk, think of you now waking,
feel our arms entwined, kneel and pick
a batch of fiddleheads, anticipate their
succulence shared with you tonight,
call the dog, and turn toward home.

STACKING WOOD

I like the way a neighbor stacks his wood
against the cold white eye of winter,
that slash of morning light that soon will
scan the bones laid bare by fall's late storms.

I like the way he's set three pallets
against the frozen ground,
each with split half moons laid flat
to anchor down the remnants of the summer,

built three square cords of sunlight
stored in shanks of beech and birch and oak
laid out in layers alternating north to south, then
east to west, each perpendicular to the last,

capped each small fortress with a tarp tied
tight against the coming snow to trap
the earth's warm breath late loping up
the mountain slope to mingle with

the heat still latent in the wood.
I like those three thick cubes, one fresh cut,
one but a year from green,
one fully cured and filled with fire.

But most I like the thin green snake
he didn't kill last summer
that left its slough of brittle skin
against the bark inside one stack,
then slithered off, almost liquid,
through the wild green grass.

VI

Music rises from the deep.
laughter pounding out a distant beat,
hammers striking anvils, faint at first,

growing into sharp metallic rings,
then smoothing out to round pulsations,
harmonic murmur, cattle lowing,

whale song spinning chants in fourths and fifths
across the mountain peaks and
reedy valleys drowned below.

Echoes bounce off the half-devoured sun
tap out melodies against the ocean's skin,
skip off currents, spiral round shafts of wind,

invade my head and chest until my very bones
vibrate as strings might pulse inside a storm
or birds sing raucous hymns before the dawn.

I sink, mere fact no longer floating,
babbling that the god bird has deserted me,
carried off my self, leaving this blank

filled with creatures,
alien at first, but then,
such sweet music.

WATER BUGS

pen spirals
across the fabric of the stream,
strange encryptions,
like Arabic
inked against a flowing scroll,
or Chinese brushstrokes
drawn on silk,
or poems etched on panes
of silver-coated glass
that tremble in the breeze
to shake loose
what's just been written
by nibs invisible
until one stops,
a black-brown lacquered
period of a sentence
come to rest against a floating leaf.

If everything is strings
vibrating,
perhaps these threads
of curlicue
inscribe a symphony
or its fragments.
But how to read them
quickly traced and disappearing
like ancient chants
of vanished monks
dispersed in incense to the sky?

And if that trout
suspended
speckled brown, red, and green

could sing,
what music would it scan
reversed upon my face
unfurled
against the passing clouds,
what measures
set aglow
inside the slowly moving
sun?

SHALLOWS

What sage gave thanks
he'd lived beyond desire,
come at last into his better self?
He never felt your hand against his arm,
caught your eye across a room, or danced
with you one summer's evening by the sea.
He never saw you shimmer
like morning on the ocean,
his hands skipping along the curves
of your hips, like seabirds riding
updrafts from eddies spun by you
spinning out your supple youth?

Perhaps he lived coherent, whole,
unmolested by that doubleness
that pesters me, spectator to my self,
split, halved, and parched, seeking
any coast where I can straddle land and sea.

I've seen the sere topography of snakes
where deserts thirst for falling strands
of liquid sky that never touch the ground,
lines inked across a sun-bleached parchment,
tails swept by wind to wistful commas,
finding no completion, just a thin hot space
where mist evaporates to dust.

Inside that void, perhaps some ancient
wrinkled text lives pure. I meander
in and out of sand and surf, one foot
planted on the edge of this green continent,
the other testing turbulence rolling from the deep,
mark the line where the tidal shelf falls off,

water darkens, and currents
pull toward foreign shores.

I watch the terns and gulls and pelicans
skim the shallows after schools of feeding fish,
I sometimes spy a porpoise slide along the shoal
rise and fall with fluid grace, shimmer in the sun,
then dive into its element, complete.

ACORNS

For weeks
hundred–year-old oaks
have lobbed a crop of acorns,
random cracks of pistols,
rifle shots, shotgun blasts
sprayed across the roof,
launched by gusts of wind,
shaken free by squirrels,
or merely lured by gravity's
dark jealousy
of whatever rises from the earth.

At first, the dog and cat would start
as at a sudden summer storm,
or when a stranger's at the door;
they've adjusted now, and even I
no longer bolt in search of prowlers,
rotted limbs, or delinquent kids
with weapons in the woods.

One gets used to most things,
sounds or silences, in most houses.

Still, something not quite grief
pesters the night, some pang
for hapless offspring
that clip the ridge cap,
tumble down the shingled slope,
and come to naught
with a ping inside my gutter.

II

My foot kicks acorns
off the grass; they scatter
all a-clatter down the drive,
a little rapids of thick brown
pebbles tumbling down the black
Macadam.

I stop to tease that word,
Macadam,
along my tongue, back to front
tapping my palate,
beginning and ending
in a rumble of lips like marbles
tumbling out of childhood,
like this litter left to pock a lawn
grown feral from inattention
to grownup chores.

The dog springs to retrieve
an unborn oak, a shell-bound
embryo of future limbs and trunk.
Having no taste for linguistics,
she teases me to try to extract it,
thrusting it clutched between her jaws,
then twists away,
calibrating the space between
my fingertips and her snout.

She repeats this play
until she tires, then drops
belly to asphalt to crack apart
the casing and crushes
the idea of a skeleton
between her teeth.

SAFE HOUSE

John Scarborough haunts this house.
He seeps through the broad pine floorboards,
wraps about the beams of winter light,
hangs in the air like incense after mass.

He came with our dial tone
late one afternoon while we were out
or inattentive or making love,
brought by a honeyed voice
sunny as dogwood, serious as clay,
persistent as kudzu, trolling by phone
from some cubicle down south,
sliding its filament of tidewater
accent through the static,
dangling sweet supplication,
fishing for one lucky bite from the lost
elusive wayward deadbeat John.

Like an abandoned sweetheart
she entreated him to call
about his delinquent account.
We erased the tape,
but the lady returned;
message followed message,
clogging the machine, invoking
John Scarborough, John Scarborough.
Month after month she persisted,
always while we were out
or inattentive or making love.

Thus he took up residence in our house.
We became the aiders and abettors,
John the outlaw, John on the lam.

John of the underground railroad,
she the pursuer of fugitive slaves.
John the Communist redistributing
Master Card's wealth. John the invisible.
John the invincible. John the transcendent.
John's libidinous disembodied virtual
self surfing the shopping channels
while we were out or inattentive
or making love, until one evening
we joined him, knocking down
shots of Captain Morgan in Anguilla,
sailing a sloop in Barbados,
tanned and untamed in Tahiti,
carving curves in the snow at Chamonix,
betting the house at Monte Carlo,
charging it all to John's account,
stepping out, inattentive, making love,
ageless, beyond loss, beyond grief,
cut free like astronauts, untethered,
lifelines severed, the paltry earth
falling away, receding, shrinking,
slipping into silence.

The calls have stopped, but John lingers.
We never betrayed him, never
put his pursuer off her false scent.
Instead, we give him this safe house
in exchange for the secrets
he whispers in the deep night about
what is possible and what is not.

ON COW WORSHIP

The bright barn-red barn
that nails down the pasture
near our ski house in Vermont
has a black and white
life-size fiberglass
cow
the owners hoist and drop
from place to place
throughout the summer.

It's a docile thing
as cows will be,
especially lifeless ones.
Now it pokes its wide flat nostrils
from a hay loft
fifteen feet above the ground,
now it stares stiff-legged and longing
in high grass through summer rain
at horses in their barns across the valley,
now brown-eyed and resigned
it watches its owners
sip merlot on their patio
by the fresh-cropped meadow.

Today we met the owner's brother,
who said they planned soon to install
real cows
to graze the hay and alfalfa.
These will bring thick clouds
of fat black flies,
moan to be milked
at four a.m.,
and drop steaming brown pies

across the rolling land
the breeze inhales
before it climbs our hill.

I thought of that poem by Gerald Stern
and wondered
if perhaps I love my cows best as
art.

CAT'S EYES

My dog's eyes stare round and moist
through most of our exchanges.
Yearning to decipher simple signs
for work or food or play,
they open in her face like
black-eyed Susans in the sun,
expressing frank desire, inviting me to joy.

The cat's slightly parted slits rise vertical
between thick slabs of yellow granite,
dark portals through which shadows barely slip,
steles ten thousand winters old.
Behind them lurks a cult of Druids
chanting secrets in the night.

My dog would be a good God-fearing
Christian, fetching tablets of holy writ,
barking out the Ten Commandments,
all the Cardinal Virtues, Lord's Prayer,
and Apostles' Creed, with never a crafty blink.

In the cat, there's something heathen and unholy,
wickedness, perhaps. I've seen him
track a bird outside the window,
jaw aquiver, chattering his primal lust,
seen him kill a mouse with cold disinterest,
disembowel it in his play, then squint
his innocence and curl his tail around my leg,
seducing me with rubs and purrs.

EARLY FOG, BROMLEY MOUNTAIN

Early fog lays down a lake
between green ridges hunched against the dawn,
Manchester Center mute beneath white foam,
I negotiating bursts of light and shade
splashing off the granite flank of the road
carved into this downward leaning mountain,
wondering as I descend if overnight
the valley sprang a leak,
some Aswan miracle, Three Gorges,
final scene from *Deliverance*,
left the town flattened and submerged.

I stare into the flat thick bed of white
and think that this must be forgiveness,
sleep beneath a fog, consciousness
not yet notched by the sun's harsh serrations,
to lie in silence, invisible to self,
deaf dog curled tight and faceless
without a whine or twitch from troubled dreams.

SEWING A POEM

I've risen before you to find the sun
newly spun and low inside the trees,
laying out the fabric of the day.
In the woods a bird tats a pattern
against a birch, threading beats
through bolts of spattered rays,
spelling out a code
twenty-five million years in the making,
intent on its task, indifferent
to my sitting in this early chill
trying to measure the slow
unfolding of the light.

The dog has wandered off, bored
by my scribbling, set its nose
to sniffing out the dew-drenched scent
a red fox draped along a fallen log
last evening, pausing once to fix the porch
with yellow eyes before it wrapped itself
in sunset and hurried on toward dusk.

Suspended in this seam
between dawn and day,
I gather in the work the morning does
to keep me stocked with cloth
I'll stitch with words, do my part
to sew a mantle against the chill.
When I'm done I'll take it to you,
still asleep, and wrap you
in the world's first light.

www.ingramcontent.com/pod-product-compliance
Lightning Source LLC
Chambersburg PA
CBHW031144090426
42738CB00008B/1210